CONTENTS

THE CHILDREN OF DAVID, OP. 37
(Five Modern Psalms)

The poems in this cantata are "modern" insofar as they belong to the past two centuries rather than to the distant past; I have called them psalms because, like the anonymous poems ascribed to David, they are hymns to the spirit of life. If one remembers that the biblical Psalms are pre-Christian, it will perhaps be easier to accept the term psalm in this broader sense.

Like the biblical Psalms, these poems are as varied and self-contradictory as life itself. They were chosen and ordered in such a way that each would seem to be an answer to its predecessor. Jeffers' cosmic view of joy is worlds apart from the deliberately naïve view of it expressed in Carl Dinklage's opening "Psalm," while his concept of strength is amplified a thousand-fold in Smart's "Song of David." The soprano solo who protested Jeffers' detachment returns in the fourth psalm to insist again upon humanity—this time that of Jesus.

In the last verse of the final poem, Hopkins' father image recalls the first of these psalms and I have used the phrase to recall its music as well. The three inner movements are also connected musically in a number of ways. While each piece can stand alone, it is my wish that the five pieces be performed as a unit whenever possible so that the cantata may perhaps fulfill its intention as a celebration of life in all its diversity.

—Kirke Mechem

Psalm

You shall go forward to greet the Lord
You shall Greet Him
As Friend if He be friend
As Father if He be father
As Teacher if he be teacher.
You shall Greet Him.
Surely some of you shall greet Him as Friend
He suffers longing for the greeting friend.
You are creator with Him of the new dawn;
Man is the eyes of the Lord,
The cup of the Blind Lord
And also the filler of the cup;
Man is the sustenance of the Lord.
God says: Ah greet me with joy, with Joyful Song;
Why have you set Me to such sad music,
That drains the Heart instead of filling it?
Why do you take my most joyful words
And chant them endlessly to no meaning
Or set them to a Dirge?
Have I not said Uplift your souls?
Is it not yet clear that he is uplifted who
    uplifts his heart unto Me?

—Carol Dinklage

Joy

Though joy is better than sorrow joy is not great;
Peace is great, strength is great.
Not for joy the stars burn, not for joy the vulture
Spreads her gray sails on the air
Over the mountain; not for joy the worn mountain
Stands, while years like water
Trench his long sides. "I am neither mountain nor bird
Nor star; and I seek joy."
The weakness of your breed; yet at length quietness
Will cover wistful eyes.

—Robinson Jeffers

The Song of David

He sang of God, the mighty source
Of all things, the stupendous force
    On which all strength depends:
From Whose right arm, beneath Whose eyes,
All period, power, and enterprise
    Commences, reigns, and ends.

The world, the clustering spheres He made,
The glorious light, the soothing shade,
    Dale, champaign, grove and hill:
The multitudinous abyss,
Where secrecy remains in bliss,
    And wisdom hides her skill.

Tell them, I AM, Jehovah said
To Moses: While Earth heard in dread,
    And, smitten to the heart,
At once, above, beneath, around,
All Nature, without voice or sound,
    Replied, "O Lord, THOU ART."

—Christopher Smart

Man Of My Own People
(The Jew to Jesus)

O Man of my own people, I alone
Among these alien ones can know thy face,
I who have felt the kinship of our race
Burn in me as I sit where they intone
Thy praises—those who, striving to make known
A God for sacrifice, have missed the grace
Of thy sweet human meaning in its place,
Thou who art of our blood-bond and our own.

Are we not sharers of thy Passion? Yea,
In spirit-anguish closely by thy side
We have drained the bitter cup and, tortured, felt
With thee the bruising of each heavy welt.
In every land is our Gethsemane—
A thousand times have we been crucified.

—Florence Kiper Frank

Pied Beauty

Glory be to God for dappled things—
    For skies of couple-colour as a brinded cow;
        For rose-moles all in stipple upon trout that swim;
Fresh-firecoal chesnut-falls; finches' wings;
    Landscape plotted and pieced—fold, fallow, and plough;
        And all trades, their gear and tackle and trim.

All things counter, original, spare, strange;
    Whatever is fickle, freckled (who knows how?)
        With swift, slow; sweet, sour; adazzle, dim;
He fathers-forth whose beauty is past change:
        Praise him.

—Gerard Manley Hopkins

Commissioned by the Onondaga Community College Choir,
Syracuse, N. Y., Donald B. Miller, Conductor

The Children of David

Psalm

CAROL DINKLAGE

KIRKE MECHEM
Op. 37, No. 1

+8 ft

12

Why have you set me to such ___ sad mu-sic, ___

Why have you set me to such ___ sad mu-sic, ___

Why have ___ you set ___ me to such ___ sad ___ mu-sic, ___

Why have you set me to such ___ sad ___ mu-sic, ___

Commissioned by the Schola Cantorum, Royal Stanton, Conductor

Joy

ROBINSON JEFFERS

KIRKE MECHEM
Op. 37, No. 2

16+8+4 ft

8 ft only

Commissioned by the Schola Cantorum, Royal Stanton, Conductor

The Song of David

CHRISTOPHER SMART

KIRKE MECHEM
Op. 37, No. 3

16+ 8 ft

46

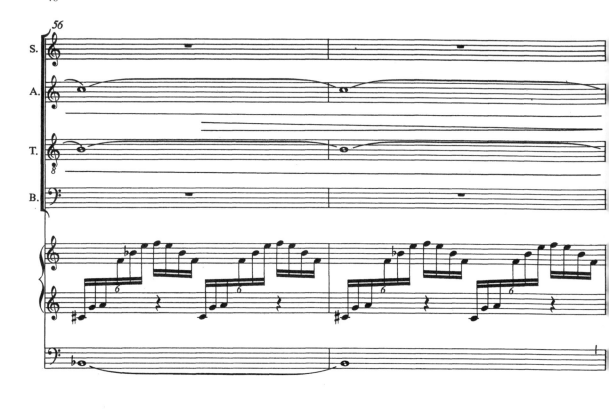

smit - ten   to   the

heart,

At   once,

a -

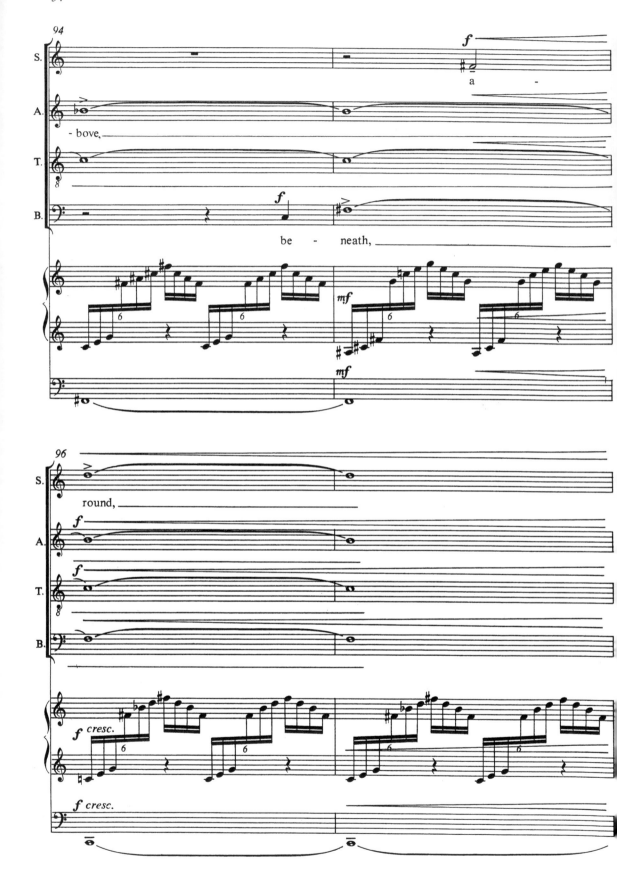

Commissioned by the Schola Cantorum, Royal Stanton, Conductor

Man of My Own People
(The Jew to Jesus)

FLORENCE KIPER FRANK

KIRKE MECHEM
Op. 37, No. 4

al - ien ones can know thy face, I who have felt the kin-ship of our race

Burn,___ burn___ in me as I sit___ where they in-tone Thy prais-es-those___ who, striv-ing to make

known A God for sac-ri-fice,___ have missed the grace___ Of thy sweet hu-man meaning in its

Commissioned by the Hartnell College Choir, Vahé Aslanian, Conductor

Pied Beauty

GERARD MANLEY HOPKINS

KIRKE MECHEM
Op. 37, No. 5

BOOSEY  HAWKES

HL48024090

DISTRIBUTED BY

ISMN 979-0-051-48488-1

ISBN 978-1-4950-9752-2